Super Snakes

John Townsend

A Hertfordshire

D0227853

Badger Publishing Limited
Oldmedow Road,
Hardwick Industrial Estate,
King's Lynn PE30 4JJ
Telephone: 01438 791037

www.badgerlearning.co.uk

2 4 6 8 10 9 7 5 3 1

Super Snakes ISBN 978-1-78147- 815-8

Text © John Townsend 2014
Complete work © Badger Publishing Limited 2014

All rights reserved. No part of this publication may be reproduced, stored in any form
or by any means mechanical, electronic, recording or otherwise without the prior
permission of the publisher.

The right of John Townsend to be identified as author of this work has been asserted
by him in accordance with the Copyright, Designs and Patents Act 1988.

Publisher: Susan Ross
Senior Editor: Danny Pearson
Publishing Assistant: Claire Morgan
Designer: Fiona Grant
Series Consultant: Dee Reid

Photos: Cover image: Image Source/REX
Page 4: Image Broker/REX
Page 5: © John Cancalosi/ardea
Page 6: Jelger Herder, Buiten-beeld/Minden Pictures/FLPA
Page 7: Michael Weber/Imagebroker/FLPA
Page 8: Image Broker/REX
Page 9: FLPA/REX
Page 10: Leon Geljon/REX
Page 11: © Jany Sauvanet/NHPA/Photoshot
Page 12: © Francois Gohier/ardea
Page 14: OsunDefender.org
Page 16: Edward Kinsman/Science Photo Library
Page 17: © John Cancalosi/Alamy
Page 18: John Pitcher/Design Pics Inc/REX
Page 19: © Daniel Heuclin/NHPA/Photoshot
Page 20: © John Cancalosi/ardea
Page 21: Franco Banfi/Solent News/REX
Page 22: IB Times + ABC News
Page 23: © Geordie Torr/Alamy
Page 24: © ChinaFotoPress/Photoshot
Page 25: © Pat Canova/Alamy
Page 26: Erik Pendzich/REX
Page 27: Jamie Hanson/Newspix/REX
Page 28: Jan Woitas/DPA/Press Association Images
Page 29: Fiona Morrison/Newspix/REX

ABERDEENSHIRE LIBRARIES	
3154108	
Bertrams	10/12/2014
J597.96	£5.99

Attempts to contact all copyright holders have been made.
If any omitted would care to contact Badger Learning, we will be happy to make appropriate arrangements.

Contents

Vocabulary

anaconda   predator

antivenom   python

fossil   taipan

milligrams   venomous

1. Fangs and venom

About 700 types of snake have special glands and fangs to inject venom into their prey.

Around 250 of these snakes can kill a human with one bite.

If you are bitten by one of these snakes you will need antivenom to save you.

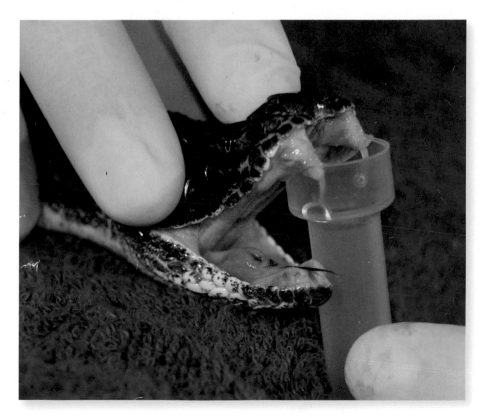

A spitting cobra sprays venom to defend itself. It aims the venom at the eyes of a predator.

King cobras are the longest snakes that inject venom. They can grow to over five metres long.

Strongest venom

The inland taipan has the strongest venom of any land snake. In one bite it can give 110 milligrams of venom. That's enough to kill about 100 humans.

So far, there are no records of anyone being killed by an inland taipan… yet!

The black mamba also has very strong venom.
It is one of the longest snakes in Africa. It is also
the fastest snake in the world – so watch out!

The most venomous snake in the world is the Belcher's sea snake. Just a few milligrams of its venom could kill 1000 people.

Watch out when you are swimming in Northern Australia!

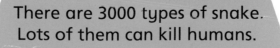

WOW! facts

There are 3000 types of snake. Lots of them can kill humans.

2. Squeezed to death

Many snakes have no venom at all. They have strong muscles instead.

That means they can crush their prey to death.

Boa constrictors hide in grass and underwater, or they hang in trees. When an animal comes by, they attack.

Large boas can swallow monkeys, pigs or deer.

Giant snakes

Anacondas are the largest snakes of South America. They can be over five metres long.

Pythons can grow to over eight metres long.

Pythons and anacondas have been known to swallow people whole (head first).

Longest snakes

Country	Name	Length
Africa	**African rock python**	**9.75 metres**
Australia	**Scrub python**	**8.5 metres**
South America	**Green anaconda**	**8.8 metres**

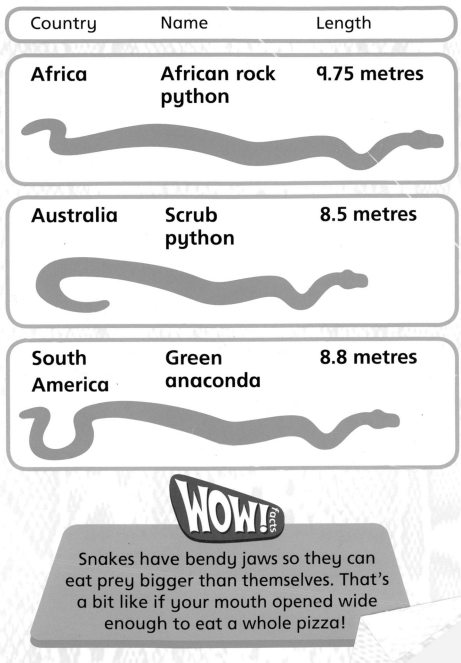

WOW! facts

Snakes have bendy jaws so they can eat prey bigger than themselves. That's a bit like if your mouth opened wide enough to eat a whole pizza!

Record breaker

In 2011, Medusa, a python, was measured at 7.67 metres long.

It was a world record for a pet snake.

It took 15 people to hold her to be measured. She weighed almost 160 kilograms.

3. Snake superpowers

Snakes are super-hunters. They don't have super eyesight but they do have super tongues.

Some snakes have very good eyesight but most can only see light and dark.

Snakes find their prey by 'sniffing' with their tongues. They have special organs in their mouths that allow them to sense warm bodies in the dark.

How do snakes grow without splitting their skin?

Snakes shed their skin
a few times a year.
They just leave their
old skin behind.
Snakeskin is made
from smooth,
dry scales.

Super skills

A snake will try
to scare off a
predator by:

- hissing
- puffing out
  a hood
- waving its
  head

But some animals will still attack snakes, even snakes with venom. A mongoose will kill and eat a deadly cobra.

The hognose snake plays dead if it is attacked. It flips onto its back with its mouth open. It stays very still and gives off a smell like rotting flesh. Most predators leave it alone and it escapes safely.

The hognose snake is a good actor!

4. Dangers to children

Some children have been attacked by snakes.

In 2007, a five-metre-long anaconda tried to eat a boy in Brazil. Matheus was playing near a river when the snake attacked from the water. As it began to strangle him, his cousin ran for help.

The boys' grandfather came just in time – with a knife. The 66-year-old man killed the snake and rushed Matheus to hospital.

After 21 stitches to repair a bite to his chest, Matheus was fine.

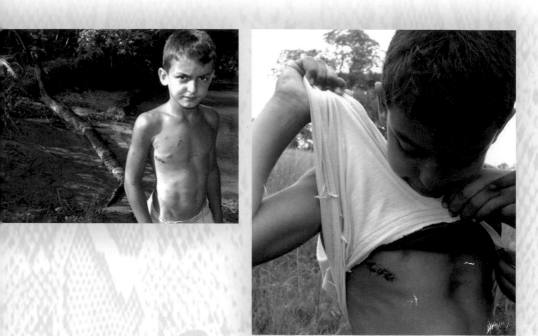

Help!

In 1999, seven-year-old Gerard O'Hare went camping with his dad in Australia.

As they slept, a python slid into the tent. It coiled around Gerard's neck and locked his head in its jaws. Luckily, Gerard's dad woke up. He fought the huge snake and threw it from the tent.

Gerard had bites to his face, shoulder and hands. He didn't want to go camping for a while after that!

This 13-year-old boy from China has a python as his best friend! Not all snakes are so friendly!

5. Snake of the past

In 2009, scientists found a fossil of a huge snake in Colombia in South America.

The snake, called Titanoboa, lived 60 million years ago. It was about twice the size of today's largest snakes – the biggest snake that ever lived.

Titanoboa was over 14 metres long, weighed more than a tonne and could swallow a large crocodile (or a few people!) in one go.

6. Snakes in the news

In the USA, lots of people keep pythons as pets.
Some of these snakes are very, very big.

If a pet python escapes it might breed with a wild snake.

Experts fear these giant snakes could give birth to a terrifying man-eating super snake.

Snake in a toilet

In 2005, in a block of flats in Manchester, a three-metre-long snake lived in the toilet pipes for three months!

People in the flats put bricks on their toilet seats to keep the snake from coming out of their toilets.

The RSPCA said snakes easily go up and down toilet pipes and would feed on rats in the sewer.

SNAKE ATTACKS ON THE RISE!

"We've got a major snake problem in this city," said a New York police officer.

"Snakes have been popping up in toilets and coming out of bathtubs."

"They are everywhere. We've been getting over 300 calls a day from people who have seen a snake in their bathroom."

Questions

How did the spitting cobra get its name? *(page 6)*

Which is the most venomous snake in the world? *(page 9)*

What was the name of the longest pet snake in the world? *(page 14)*

How do snakes find their prey? *(page 16)*

Which animal can kill and eat a snake? *(page 19)*

Has this book changed the way you feel about snakes?

Index